T0031617

PUT YOUR YOUR BIG GIRL PANTS ON...

and other POWER MOVES to INCREASE INFLUENCE

MEG BUCARO

Put Your Big Girl Pants On

©2023 Meg Bucaro

ISBN 979-8-35093-698-8

eBook ISBN 979-8-35093-699-5

CONTENTS

DEDICATION

This book is dedicated to my incredible family.

To my daughter who I hope will always believe in her value she brings to the world. You were in my mind during every chapter. I pray you will maintain your ability to self-advocate, (maybe sometimes less sass would be welcome) and that you will never shrink to make others more comfortable. Keep your feistiness and balance it with sincere openness to others. You amaze me and I could not be prouder of you. Your communication skills are incredible and will take you far in life, I promise!

To my oldest son, who has taught me about a gentler way of communication, where peace and understanding is always possible, even when stressed or anxious. I hope you will continue to lift up those around you and provide an example to others what sincere understanding of each other looks like. Most importantly, I pray you grow to fully understand the amazing value you bring to your relationships. Continue to be comfortable in your own skin, flashing your smirky smile that lights up my entire heart! You always bring a beautiful tenderness and kindness to those around you. I continue to learn so much from you!

To my youngest son, who seems to have no problem being heard in our household. Your humor and energy fuel me. Remember, those who know, don't tell. Keep soaring, pushing and stay humble. You asked me to insert the phrase, 'son-of-a biscuit' into this manuscript but I am not that creative. So there ya' go! (See what I did there?!?!). Keep your spirit, your enthusiasm for life. See the women in your life and be an ally to help others find and amplify their voice.

To my parents, who have shown me, by the way in which they live their lives, that doing things the right way, is the only way. Thank you for showing me anything is possible and to self-advocate when shit ain't right. Thank you for not grounding me when my report cards came home with checkmarks under "talks too much during class." Thank you for showing me that I too, can own a thriving business and build it into whatever I desire. Thank you for showing me how to dream, work hard and trust the mystery.

Lastly, this book would not exist without my husband's encourage-ment and ongoing support. He knew this book was in me, even when I doubted. When the printer died, I missed deadlines, or I became too stressed to participate in family matters during the writing of this book. Thank you for loving me unconditionally, every day. You have shown me what love truly is and I do not have the words to express my immense gratitude for your belief in me. Your love makes me a better human being. I love you. Thank you!

WHY THIS BOOK?
WHY NOW?

Dear fellow bad ass, who secretly doubts herself at times,

I know, it can be rough, cruel and soul crushing. When you desire, from the depths of your heart to feel like a successful confident woman, who maybe can't always find the right words or actions for every situation, but strives to grow and improve nonetheless. Your desire for greatness comes from deep within. Maybe this desire burns from generations of bad ass women, in their own right, or maybe you are breaking a cycle that only you were meant to break.

You may have visions of where you want to be, how you want to feel, walking in to a situation with a healthy self-confidence, not ego or fakeness, but true belief in yourself and your abilities.

You envision entering professional or personal situations with your own self-confidence, feeling good about your responses to others' questions and offering ideas that are smart.

Or maybe you can't envision what your specific success looks like yet. But this greatness lies inside you and you feel it pop up, every now and then.

Maybe you just are not there quite yet. You are not sure how to get there, what program, coach, outfit change, or workout program you need in order to feel like you could conquer the world. And yet, it is there, waiting to completely take over and transport you to the land of feeling like a self-assured woman who is kicking ass and taking names.

You see, you badass, I have been waiting for you. Or maybe I have been waiting for the opportunity to reach out to you. Life continues to throw curve balls at us. Sometimes, we see it coming, then duck. Other-times, we do not see the nasty turn it takes as we swing and strike out.

We may not see the old boys club (or PTO Mom's club) before we are excluded from it.

We may not see the rejection before it hits us.

We may not anticipate the setback before it blocks our path.

We may not have anticipated the wage or confidence gaps.

We may not see the mean girls coming, no matter how old you may be.

… Or the insults, back handed compliments, unwanted sexual comments or advances.

But here we are. We live in a world where all of this and more exists that can easily block our path to success, however we choose to define our own success, personal or professional. And yet, we are not giving up or giving in. We have so much to offer the world we can't, won't and shouldn't stop.

SO, WHY THIS BOOK? WHY NOW?

I applied for a position once, in an organization where I already had a different position. According to the people who were close to the hiring process, I had a great chance of getting this job. I was shocked to get a generic email from Human Resources advising me I did not get the job. I knew the job was never guaranteed to me, but I knew I was very qualified and had the experience they sought in a candidate. This was a shock to my system, to be candid.

I asked for feedback from the appropriate people. The most senior man in charge agreed to provide feedback and through his assistant we arranged a meeting for the next morning. He was in charge of this entire department. I had worked under his overall direction for the past 10 years so while we knew each other he did not have a hand in my daily work responsibilities. However, after he showed up 10 minutes late, he began to share his insight.

Without posing a question, he immediately began to inform me that I needed to give 120% just not 100%, without providing a single example. He explained that in the Olympics, only one gold medal gets earned and that this position was much like the Olympic competition. He spoke in such general terms, while I documented his comments, I felt like this was a prank. He could have given this feedback to *anyone* that applied for *any* job in the organization, *ever*. I graciously and politely ended the meeting to get to my next meeting.

I was quite upset. *This* was why I did not get the job? I was completely underwhelmed and partly insulted by his 'feedback.' However, he was the highest position that I could answer to about this process. So, I slept on it.

Two weeks later, I received feedback from one of his direct reports who was much more familiar with my work than he was. She provided a specific piece of constructive feedback which I very much appreciated. We then started to talk about the entire process and the feedback her superior gave me. She appeared dumbfounded. As we laughed about a few comments that was communicated to me, she wanted to brainstorm about any positions I may be interested in. However, I stopped her, politely. I was not interested. I firmly believed (and was proven right) that this position was clearly not meant for me in that moment. So, I reiterated,

"I applied for this position. I did not get it. I asked for feedback. I got it. And now, I am going to pull up my big girl pants, and move on." It took me some time to process that rejection, but I promised myself, I would only use that experience to get stronger and more successful. Don't get me wrong, I was crushed when I did not get that job. I felt rejected and 'not good enough', among my colleagues whom I worked alongside for a decade. I wanted to use this experience to benefit other women who have ever experienced this idea not feeling worthy enough. I also knew these feelings of rejection were temporary and that I could and would pick myself up, leaning on my communication expertise to set myself up for the right opportunities I had yet to experience. I knew this because like you, I have lived it, we all have, through various life stages, highs and lows.

Now, this book has been in the making for years! With a Master's Degree in Communication Studies, original academic research on gender differences in communication of confidence, and as higher education faculty for the past 20+ years, I have always known that how we show up to others, impacts our future. In 2009, I decided to help those who may not know how exactly to present their best self to others and launched my business where I coach individuals, train teams and speak to audiences about how to utilize communication skills to show up as the best version of themselves.

I'd like you to use this book as a hand book. Pick it up, read for a few minutes, Put it down. Bend the page (gasp!) or not and pick it back up. This book is not a thick book, and was designed this way on purpose. Busy women do not need to read 500-page books to learn how to show up powerfully. In here, I will supply you with ideas, tactics, strategies and techniques to test out. Some will work more fluidly than others for you, specifically. There are no guarantees when we talk about the science and art of communication. However, stacking the cards in your favor includes adaptation of potentially new, more effective behaviors and ways of thinking.

Let this book be a call to arms to fight the self-doubt, rejection, or stumbling blocks that have stopped or slowed you down from pursuing what you know is your future success. The world will continue to throw difficult situations at us, but we must promise ourselves, to utilize the tools we have to push ourselves towards whatever our definition of success is and fight like hell to stay on that path. Then, when we reflect and look back on our journey, we help those who are in earlier stages of a similar journey.

That is why this book and why now. Like you, I have been beaten down by the pressures of the world on my shoulders. As a business owner, employee, mother, wife, daughter, sister, friend, volunteer; there is no end to the challenges. No seriously, there will always be challenges.

But with the right tools we can overcome such challenges and dare to use them to push forward to our own success.

Join me as I walk through the tools that have helped me so far as I reveal the secrets behind showing up confidently, authentically in pursuit of your best life.

CHAPTER 1:

WHAT'S COMMUNICATION GOT TO DO WITH IT?

(#WINK TINA TURNER)

You may be wondering, how communication behaviors play such an integral role in our personal success? The answer is simple. Communication experts explain that we spend 80%[1] of our working day in some form of communication. Yet, of this 80%, we only spend approximately 15% involved in purposeful communication. This means, that while we spend most of our day communicating, we are intentional about it for just a small fraction of that time. Instead of looking at this negatively, I prefer to look at the wide opportunity we now have. This means that throughout most of our day, we can take more control, particularly when communicating with others who can influence our professional or personal journey. Most of our day now becomes opportunity, every day, to show up as the best version of our self and communicate with intention. The most unnerving problem about this is that we are mostly unaware of the judgements that are happening around us due to how we interact with others. Remember this is true in our personal and professional lives. You may be curious as to how this can happen, day in and day out.

Think of the last time you hopped into your car and headed out to a familiar destination. Possibly it was the grocery store, work, school, a friend's home, local hangout or a favorite restaurant. You may have begun moving towards your destination, lost yourself in thought or got wrapped up in your favorite 90s rap lyrics *(I do not blame you!)*. You soon arrived without much recollection of exactly how you got there. You do not recall specific stop lights, corners or traffic patterns that you encountered along the way. It was as if you drove on autopilot.

Autopilot mode tends to happen when we do something so often, we do not have to lend much critical thought to complete the process. Of course, if there was an object in your way, or construction blockages, you would have thoughtfully maneuvered around, possibly picking a new route analyzing your options. However, if everything stayed the same as you expected, you would not have had to think critically along your way.

We also operate like this when we breathe. We typically do not critically think about breathing, we just do it. This is the case until we struggle to breathe, like during an asthma issue, illness, anxiety attack or strenuous exercise. We begin to think more about the intricate details of driving or breathing when it becomes challenging.

This simplification of a familiar process (autopilot) happens in our brain and is meant to help us. It has to do with what scientists discovered in the 1990s, called the "default mode network," which is a set of brain regions that plays a crucial role in such autopilot behavior.[2] It is as if our brain switches to cruise control. This is often the reason why we may answer the wrong greeting question, like "Hey, what's going on?" and then answer "good" since we are so accustomed to hearing a different greeting like "How's it going?"

While not always helpful on accuracy, operating on autopilot helps to makes us more efficient at tasks without having to expend too much brain power. This is so especially when the tasks are extremely predictable and common. Driving, breathing, or performing a game we are good at becomes second nature so we can complete the task while utilizing less of our brain. However, what happens when our brain switches to default mode or cruise control and it begins to hurt us?

Most humans experience autopilot while communicating. It is common to not think about preparing any form of communication unless it is considered important and out of the norm. Think of why we seem to prepare for a formal presentation, a difficult conversation or a job interview more than we do for a team meeting, the school open house evening, average patient interaction, meeting with colleagues or during book club interactions where we do not think much about it ahead of time.

Every day, we are speaking, listening, typing, posting, reading, responding or sending nonverbal signals to those around us. Our day is full of communication situations. Too often I hear from women that they just don't understand why they are not getting that promotion, the ideal relationship they seek, or the respect they believe they deserve. When everything else adds up, I direct them to focus on how they show up. Examining how others experience us in any given communication situation is what I call 'showing up'. While communication theories have proven that our appearance is important in social perceptions, it is the totality of the words we say and how we say them that matter greatly. Additionally, what we say while communicating provides examples to others on our intelligence, experience, how we view ourselves, how healthy our self-esteem is, what we are willing to put up with, and where our boundaries lie. The problem is as humans, our natural inclination is to leave most of our communication to chance. We trust ourselves that whatever is needed at the time, will fly out of our mouths when necessary. This happens when we are operating on autopilot in any given communication situation.

Think of the last time someone said something to you that took you off guard. Possibly you were not prepared for that particular comment. Since you were unsure as to what to say in that moment, you may have let it slide, said something you regretted, stayed quiet when you did not intend to, and wished you knew exactly what to say or do in that instance. You said nothing but you wanted to, you just were not sure how to respond, so you didn't.

Staying quiet when we have something to say is the most dangerous thing we as women can do. #Speakup

Staying quiet when we have something to say, ensures that our political offices, board rooms, surgical rooms, courtrooms and industries like construction, law enforcement, technology, startups and financial services continue to be dominated by men. And while we need men in these positions, we need more women there, especially now! When we stay quiet, take up less space and devalue our contribution, we send a message that we do not think we are enough. We communicate that we are less valuable than our male counterparts. When in fact, we match men in our education, expertise, and often have greater capacity for more effective communication.

Communication is the key for women. #communicationiskey #communicateourvalue

There is a lot happening in a woman's brain during any communication situation. We have heard that men are from Mars and women are from Venus however, that only scratches the surface on gender differences when it comes to how we communicate.

Frankly, women are better at receiving and interpreting body language. In fact, when processing messages, women use 16 different parts of their brain while men only use seven parts. [3] Women do not only hear the words that are spoken, but our brains immediately take in context and outside variables like tone of voice, posture, movement, and facial expressions at a rapid pace. In fact, women's brains are much more effective at this than men's brains. I remind my husband of this fact, regularly. He just loves that.:-)

Sure, my focus may naturally gravitate towards the nuances of communication skills. My husband is then subject to discussions about why he did not pick up on the nonverbal cues during the conversations of which we are both involved. As I further my research, I realized, one explanation may just be that my brain is simply pre-determined to process all of the cues being sent our way more effectively.

When working with female law enforcement professionals, I have explained why they are naturally better than their male counterparts on surveying the entire communication situation in a moment's notice, thanks to neuroscience. Females are actually at an advantage with how quickly our brains intercept multiple communication variables in milliseconds. In fact, there is enough research to say that women are superior in 'interpreting facial expressions cross culturally: it's a universal attribute."[4]

There is no better example of this, than the stereotypical joke referencing a husband taking his wife's word that she is "fine" when in fact, her tone, facial expressions and posture will indicate otherwise. Of course, we know she was pissed but the goofy husband in this joke, had no idea what he did wrong.

While women process all of these expressive inputs, we use the information we gather to react. Our brains are quite busy. We quickly determine what the words mean and what the nonverbal signals are communicating. We naturally try to determine if there are any inconsistencies between the verbal and non-verbal to determine the true meaning. We then think through the context of this particular communication situation. Then, our neurons work hard to figure out what conclusions we can draw before we decide how we should react. This process takes mere seconds.

Ladies, we were *made* for this process of communication! #womensbrainsareamazing

So, while we are walking around on auto pilot, we are actually cutting ourselves short, every single day. We are not taking advantage of the opportunities we have to communicate our value, our ideas, our capabilities or our boundaries. What is mind-blowing is that this is not overly difficult. This is not arduous. Taking advantage of communication techniques that allow you to show up in all of your power can be exhilarating. You have the power. It starts with awareness that you will find in this book. Then it continues with a commitment to exercise the communication muscles more regularly. This book will give you the tools but most importantly it will take a strong belief in yourself to continuously show up as the best version of yourself. No matter what tricks you may learn and hone, you will only appear inauthentic if you do not speak from the depths of what you firmly believe about yourself.

You deserve to have a seat at that table. You deserve to earn that promotion. You deserve to be in a healthy, loving relationship. You deserve the chance to improve your work shift or schedule. You deserve to be treated respectfully and lovingly. You deserve to not be talked to disrespectfully. You deserve to say no without the guilt. You deserve to sit down every now and then and put your feet up. You have already earned the ability to decide what you want to do and be. Believe that. Believe in yourself. And if you are not there yet, commit yourself to taking a journey of self-belief. People can smell inauthenticity miles away. And while there is something to 'fake it until you make it,' it only goes so far.

I am asking you, before you dedicate yourself to improving your communication behaviors, to believe in yourself and your ability to intentionally communicate exactly as you desire. Learning a handful of important communication tools, will help to open your eyes to some phrases that will greatly help you in tough meetings, social circles, relationships, annoying social situations, or tough conversations with certain colleagues. But first, you must believe in your ability. Period. Because if you do not, who will?

So, you see, not only do we have gobs of opportunity to show up exactly as we'd like, each and every day, we are also perfectly set up to manage communication situations. So, think about what would you like to accomplish with this new-found communication prowess? I have written this book so you can feel:

- unapologetically comfortable in your own skin
- confident in your ability
- unabashedly and authentically you
- self-assured in what you have to give to the world
- apathy for the haters because you *know* they are missing out
- proud of yourself, without excuses or qualifiers
- excited for what lies ahead of you
- limitless on what you want to accomplish
- success, on *your* terms, however you define it

Life is going to get us down, every now and then. We will doubt ourselves. We will knock ourselves down, throw a pity party, and sit in our own puddle of tears. Then, we will put our big girl pants on, lift up our chins, dust off our shoulders, take a breath, get up and move forward, damn it! Feeling self – assured is not about everything going right in your life all the time. In fact, it is quite the opposite.

In those moments of highs and lows, how you show up, how you talk to yourself and how you communicate with others, will determine your next step on the path to your success!

Utilize the opportunities you have to increase your awareness of how you can present yourself as powerfully and influential as you'd like. Let me ask, when was the last time you felt good in your own skin, feeling truly comfortable, authentic and confident? Dare I say proud of yourself? No matter how you are feeling, you *can* communicate with power and confidence. You *can* show up authentically you. You *can* present yourself as the best version of yourself. Now, let your mind wander, if this was possible... how would your life be different?

I'd like you to consider taking a step forward on the path to powerful communication to see how this can increase your success. The following chapters will outline small actions and habits that will help women show up as their best self, whether they feel that way or not, in any communication situation.

Women are equally qualified to achieve their personal success, but where we differ greatly, is our communication. This book is for the woman who, underneath all of her busyness of life, dares to dream of more. She is confident that she can level up and accomplish all that she desires once she becomes more aware of how she shows up in the world. By taking control of her communication behaviors, rarely having to second guess what she should say in a particular situation and feeling quite sure of herself in any situation where her voice is necessary and greatly needed, is within her reach.

Ladies, it is time to dream big and work towards whatever definition you use for success. There are specific strengths and challenges that women possess when it comes to communication. There are equally specific solutions and behaviors that women can adopt as their own to thrive as their most confident and authentic self.

ACTION ITEMS:

1. Reflect on what you would like to accomplish with this new found, communication prowess?

2. How would your life be different if you had the confidence you desire, in common communication situations? Visualize yourself tackling these situations with confidence and ease.

CHAPTER 2:

JUDGEMENTS — THEY ARE ALL AROUND US!

Imagine, you walk in to a meeting where a notorious colleague is gearing up to avoid work that should be in her purview. You always seem to be the one who ends up with her work. But this day, you walk in, quieter than usual. You enter the meeting room confidently. Calmly. Calculated. You hold back your smile for a moment but sincerely greet each attendee. When the work in question is brought up, you already have a plan. You begin by asking your prepared questions that guide the conversation to the point that this particular colleague is truly the right person for this work load due to her experience and expertise. You have complimented this person on previous work as you tied examples into your explanation. She is smiling. You are well paced, a bit reserved in your demeanor. You are determined. You have practiced the phrases, "I would love to help but this time I just cannot." And you have prepared your reasoning that is based on facts and logic alone, just in case your supervisor pushes. But they don't.

Sure, you communicate firmly with your words but what spoke louder than words were your expressive behaviors.

Maybe that situation is not realistic for you but if you have ever experienced a job interview, a first date, or meeting 'the parents' for the first time, you likely have experienced the role of first impression, based mostly on expressive behaviors. Not only are these judgements made in mere seconds, they can last for the long haul. We have learned that it is quite difficult to reverse a first impression judgement. Likely that is where the phrase 'You never get a second chance to make a good first impression' originates. While we may know this, intellectually, how often do you really reflect on how social judgements of others affect your interactions and outcomes, thus your success?

As the late Dr. Nalini Ambady, a social scientist who was a well-known professor at Harvard University for her focus on expressive behaviors and judgements, states, "The way in which people move, talk, and gesture-their facial expressions, posture and speech-all contribute to the formation of impressions about them. Many of the judgements we make about others in our everyday life are based on cues from these expressive behaviors"[5]

Since we spend the majority of our day in some form of communication, most of our day becomes opportunity, every day, to show up as our best self. Are your expressive behaviors communicating this?

The most unnerving problem about this is that we are mostly unaware of the judgements that are happening about us due to how we interact with others. Remember this is true in our personal and professional lives.

Similar research done by Dr. Ambady, found that surgeon's malpractice history was accurately postdicted by researchers based alone on their tone of voice with patients during 20 seconds of an audio clip. The study found that doctors with perceived higher dominance were more likely to be sued in the past. This was determined in what Ambady and her team called "thin slices" of time, twenty seconds to be exact here.

What do you communicate by your tone of voice, in a mere 20 seconds?

Another study looked at thin slice judgements of physical therapists and geriatric patients in 20-second video clips over a 3-month time period. It was found that positive facial expressions of the therapists positively correlated with short – and long-term function of their patients. If the therapist had more positive facial expressions, their patients improved their functioning.

What do your facial expressions say to others... in 20-second increments?

Our movements are just as important when it comes to how others judge us. One study showed that students could determine "biased from unbiased teachers" from brief clips of classroom behaviors.[6] What do others say about you as they watch you (not in a freaky way, of course) in a thin slice of time?

Too often, we underestimate the role of our communication behaviors. While we spend a majority of our time in some form of communication we may not actively pay attention to the fact that we are often judged by our nonverbal behaviors. Nonverbal language, also known as body language include facial expressions, eye contact, tone of voice, posture, gestures, movement, rate of speech, and any movement that transfers meaning. When we learn that only 10-15% of our communication is done intentionally, we realize that while we are open to social judgements most of our day, we rarely make an intentional effort to ensure we remain in control of the messaging we intend to send to others.

Bottom line: others are making judgements of our expressive behaviors that we mostly do not think much about in our interactions. We can influence others by our expressive behaviors if we know how.

If we become increasingly aware of the many chances we have to present ourselves exactly as we intend, we may understand how much opportunity for control we actually possess. This is the case even in the most unexpected situations. I coached a detective who was to testify in a criminal trial. We explored her presence in the courtroom. We worked on ways to show up, immediately and intentionally, even in the most unexacting moments. Of course, it is safe to say that most of the judgements will happen inside the courtroom so we work on preparation, body language and questioning from the defense. However, we also explore the lesser-attended-to moments. The moment she parks her car in the parking lot, she knew any jurors could be watching. The way she walked, smiled or not, while walking into the courthouse was all under her control. She just had to be aware of it. When she became aware of the possible audition in the parking lot, lobby, bathroom or hallways in which she was participating, she took control by carefully choosing her movements, facial expressions and even greetings to all she met on her way into the courtroom. She never knew exactly who she might run in to and who might have the verdict of the case in their hands. Perceptions are important.

For example, while women are better at interpreting nonverbal language, we are not superior when it comes to communicating power. Women can undermine their power and credibility by exhibiting tentative non-verbal behaviors and showing deference. Women may be attempting to express themselves assertively but then cancel the effort. This occurs when trying to soften the blow by saying one thing and doing another, like unwarranted nervous giggling or punctuating a serious sentence with a smile [7] or question mark tone, aka, upspeak.

A WARNING

Significant research has also been conducted on the congruency of messaging between our verbal and non-verbal communication. The link between expressing a certain sentiment verbally and ensuring that your non-verbal behaviors agree with that sentiment will benefit you. Studies found that when there is a lack of congruency, people default to believing our non verbals more than the words we actually express.[8] This is demonstrated when we hear someone say that they are 'fine' but we know by their tone of voice or eye roll, that they are not in fact 'fine'. What is even more telling is that "people who exhibit behavioral inconsistency are likely to elicit negative evaluations." When the words we say, are inconsistent with how we say them, social judgements lean quite negatively towards us.

BOTTOM LINE:
PEOPLE TRUST US LESS WHEN
OUR WORDS AND ACTIONS DO NOT LINE UP.

This was never more obvious than when I witnessed a new chief of police take the helm, after his well-liked predecessor, left the position. The new chief created a video to share online introducing himself. In the welcome video, he desired to assure the community that though the Chief of Police had changed hands, the department was still very open to the community. He invited the viewers to stop by the police department with any questions or concerns. The issue was during this entire video, he kept his hands clasped in front of his midsection. His voice was monotone without much variation. His nonverbal language did not come off welcoming or sincere. His words expressed an 'openness' and a 'welcoming' but his body language did not communicate that once, during this entire video. Although this individual was known to be extremely intelligent and had a long tenure in law enforcement, the public did not like him as much as his predecessor and he moved out of the department within the year.

Therefore, you see the study of social judgment is not just a matter of making a good first impression but one that should cause us all to increase our awareness of how we all make social judgements. This should cause us to examine if what we say and how we say it are congruent. We can also use this knowledge as a tool to guide our pursuit of success. If we know more about how social perceptions are garnered from our body language, then we can be better prepared.

What does this mean for *you*, the reader? If you are sending messaging that others are judging, but you are not fully aware; this means that you have no idea of those social judgements, which are likely impacting your success, personal or professional.

Tip: We must understand how social judgements are made and use it to our advantage.

For example, I was interviewing for a position where I knew it was all 50-year-old men. I selected my outfit based on what I knew of men their age/stage of life. I knew that men saw bright colors as warm and caring but weak, at times. The job I was seeking needed firm leadership. I wore a navy-blue suit. Were they going to judge me based on my appearance? Oh, hell yes, they were. It is human nature. Did I want to take full control over what it was I wore? Yes, I did. Of course, we can take this to any extreme and I am not saying that we must look at our color pallets in our closest every day. My point here is that if we know we will be judged, why not use that information to help us succeed? (Psst, I got the job.)

Think about how you develop a view with someone you work. What do you think of them? How did you settle on those opinions of them as a person, as a supervisor, colleagues, etc.? Now, are you aware of the social judgements made about you? How do you know they exist?

Our facial expressions, tone of voice or body movements can communicate a myriad of messages. We can tell someone if we are happy, frustrated, if we like the person speaking or trust them, all without saying one word. The biggest surprise may be that most of this expressive behavior is unintended, subconscious, and yet extremely effective. In fact, Harvard researchers found that these expressive behaviors as social cues, are neither "encoded or decoded at an intentional, conscious levels of awareness" but that they have "great communicative power."

Our expressive behaviors predict interpersonal outcomes.[9] Do you know of someone who always seems to get herself into similar situations? Being treated as a doormat at work? Or in her love life? Allowing others to persuade her to do things she really does not want to do? Working longer hours than she really wants to but does not know how to stop? Does she do 'most of the work at home' because no one will listen to her? These are all situations that can be improved with the right communication, including but not limited to expressive behaviors. We have great communicative power and opportunity with our expressive behaviors. We must begin to consider any communication situation as an audition, of which we can always show up as our best self.

ACTION ITEMS:

1. Spend half of a day, becoming more aware of potential social judgments of you, during a normal work day. Is your supervisor interacting with you? Clients? Students? Colleagues? The general public? Based on the first two minutes of your interaction- determine what judgments might be happening of you.

2. Think of the day head, what interactions might you have, where judgements can be made? Be intentional about all decisions which need to be made. What decisions can you make to take control over some of the social judgements? Walking down the hallway. Your presence in a Zoom meeting. Your informal conversation in the bathroom. Your big presentation. Are you showing up as you intend?

CHAPTER 3:

WHY ARE WE TALKING ABOUT CONFIDENCE?

I was waiting for the potential client to welcome me into his office to discuss my training programs for his staff. It would be my first multi-program contract and I was feeling the nerves! Minutes away from entering the meeting to pitch my "Increase Your Influence through Body Language" training program, I took stock of how nervous I appeared. Bringing my awareness to my body language, I realized I had my legs crossed so tightly that my muscles were twitching. My posture was unintentionally slouched. My arms were crossed, resting on my legs. I looked small, unsure of myself as if I did not believe I belonged there. This was a problem given the reason I was invited to this meeting. Snapping out of then negative self-talk hole I was digging for myself, I took a deep breath and focused on what I could control, which was how I was showing up, physically. I knew I had to communicate credibility, competence and confidence. Knowing that my program was about influencing others via body language, I quickly adjusted my posture to reframe my body into appearing confident and self-assured. I adjusted my breathing so any adrenaline spike did not work its way into my extremities shown by a shaky voice or hands. I internally reminded myself of my qualifications and sincere ability to train his staff well. Moments later, the soon-to-be-client walked into his waiting room and greeted me. Days later, I would find that this became my biggest contract thus far.

WHY IS CONFIDENCE PART OF THIS EQUATION?

As you may imagine, it is much easier and more advantageous to demonstrate powerful communication behaviors if you have some semblance of self-confidence. But first let's define what confidence actually is. Confidence has been viewed as:

- feeling of self-assurance arising from one's appreciation of one's own abilities or qualities.[10]

- Confidence means feeling sure of yourself and your abilities — not in an arrogant way, but in a realistic, secure way.[11]

- is a belief in oneself, the conviction that one has the ability to meet life's challenges and to succeed—and the willingness to act accordingly?[12]

- belief that you can accomplish what you set out to do.[13]

HOW DOES THIS MAKE A DIFFERENCE IN WOMEN'S LIVES?

Confidence is the only mental attribute that can enhance physical capabilities like power, strength, and speed. When you are confident, you perform at a higher level than when you don't hold your abilities in high regard.[14] And while there is a gray area when discussed confidence and power, for now, think of confidence as something you control while power is something that others must perceive. This is good news, you have the ability to work on your level of confidence. While this book is not taking on the complete analysis of self-confidence, it does highlight how confidence is tied to how we show up, our presence. This is especially important when we show up to communication situations where others' judgments of us will affect our personal or professional success.

Confidence is important for everyone, regardless of gender, as it is a key factor in achieving success and personal fulfillment. No matter what stage in life or daily activities in which you are involved, the value of confidence cannot be understated.

Confidence is especially important for women to possess as we are judged in many circumstances, and often before we even open our mouths. #Confidenceiskey

Confidence in yourself means being sure of your own value, capacity, and ability regardless of the opinions of those whom surround you. Confidence[15] helps women in particular to increase credibility, likability, influence and frankly, to live the best version of our lives. Yet, there is a problem...and it is twofold:

1. A confidence gap exists between men and women. Spoiler alert: men are found to have more confidence than women. This gap is shown to exist through every stage of life.[16] And likely not a surprise, it is very easy to assess a confident person from their communication behaviors as their true feelings leak out to others as they communicate. Individuals who feel confident, will naturally have nonverbal language behaviors that show confidence.

2. Research also tells us that our true feelings and attitudes leak out of us, thus unintentionally showing others how we really feel.[17] So, when we don't feel confident, our self-doubt leaks out of us. Remember how nervous I felt in the client's waiting room? I

subconsciously made myself smaller and therefore appeared less confident in appearance. You may recognize this emotional leakage as nervous gesturing, physically making yourself smaller, a shaky voice, placing your arms crossed against your midsection, a lack of eye contact or a myriad of other low-power body language elements.

We already heard in the previous chapter how easily social perceptions are formed by our non-verbal behavior. Presenting ourselves with a lack of confidence is incredibly risky for women who want to progress in their career, self-advocate, get the sale, or simply influence anyone...ever... about anything. If women feel less confident than men, and their feelings leak out of them, it becomes part of their communication style, a style that expresses a lack of confidence. I wonder if *this* is the reason we see more men in positions of power. Not because men have more experience, education, drive, capacity or talent, but because they consistently show up with more confidence. This does not mean that the systemic bias in support of men and against women does not exist but I argue that more women presenting themselves with confidence can only help. Focusing on how we show our level of confidence, competence and self-assuredness is one tool which we can use easily, just by increasing our awareness of how and what our emotional leakage communicates to others.

Bestselling author and leadership expert, John C. Maxwell states, "Confidence in oneself is the cornerstone of leadership."[18] The communication of confidence is a foundational skill for any woman who seeks to not only serve in a position of leadership but to find any level of her own personal success. In fact, the term executive presence is not describing executive's desired behavior. Executive presence does not exist without confidence.

And if you are a little uncomfortable or not as interested in 'leadership' in the formal sense, I urge you to think of a time you had any influence over someone else without leadership. It does not matter if you are seeking to influence your child, a retail store manager, a supervisor, your internet provider, an interviewing committee or a potential client, showing up more confidently will only benefit you.

The role of confidence in our communication style is likely the most overlooked skill that dramatically affects how others view and ultimately judge us.

When you feel more confident you look more confident. When you look more confident, others perceive you as confident. If we possess a healthy (not egotistical) self-confidence, it often shows up clearly to others and influences how others view us. There's a scientific reason why we are attracted to confidence. We're social beings, so we look for cues from our environment on how to act, and cues from others on how we should treat them. That's why confident body language is often inherently trustworthy: relaxed shoulders, stillness, (or lack of fidgeting), maintained eye contact, and hands out where you can see them. It's built to instill trust in your abilities, and when you trust yourself, you give others the message that you're worth their trust too.[19]

In many situations, presenting yourself confidently provides benefits that have positive consequences. Candidly, people who demonstrate self-confident behavior:

- Receive more positive evaluations from others.

- Are seen as more well-liked.

- Are chosen more often as potential partners, in speed dating, as romantic partners who flirt (a confident behavior).

- Are viewed as more trustworthy.

Interacting in a self-confident manner has beneficial consequences on a person's personal and professional life that include but are not limited to, speed-dating and job success, particularly in sales performance.[20]

If we continue to pay little attention to how we show up, how our bodies communicate messaging to others, we may unintentionally place ourselves at a disadvantage. When these 'others' are decision makers or anyone who has influence over your life, this is a cycle that can provide quite a challenge for women who are trying to succeed. Whether we are climbing the corporate ladder, running our own business, spending our days with dependents at home, volunteering, working the second shift or anything we damn well please – all women can benefit from presenting herself with confidence.

Now, at this point you may be thinking, "This confidence thing seems a bit overwhelming, I mean how I am supposed to feel confident all of the time." My answer? You're not. As self-assured as many women are, it is nearly impossible to feel ultimate confidence in all areas of our life, all the time. Notice, I am encouraging confidence, I am also encouraging taking control of our communication behaviors but not once will I say you must feel confident all of the time.

Tip: Become more aware of the messages you send.

Is it doable to think that we can become more aware of the messages we send, nonverbally? The purpose is not to inflate our ego but more ethically, for expansion of our best selves, demonstrate confident nonverbal body language. We are all succeeding at something. We all have a very specific gift to share with the world. We know it deep down, but at times, we allow self-doubt, an uneasiness and negative self-talk to protect us from expanding too much. I mean, what if we fail and embarrass ourselves? It is just so much easier and comfy cozier to stay small. But at what cost? When we consistently settle to give up self-expansion and stop pushing ourselves just out of our comfort zone we are not allowing our gift to reach all those who need it most! The world needs you to show up, stand up, and confidently self-advocate to accomplish all which you desire.

Maybe the world needs your solution to a problem, your kindness, expertise or maybe your family needs the financial security, or your children just need to witness your confidence. The problem is that too often, we believe that we are not good at certain aspects of communication (i.e. public speaking, difficult conversation, confrontations, etc.). Or we decide we are too self-conscious to try to improve that part of our communication skills. Both circumstances encourage us to give up control of what our future could be!

When we show up feeling confident in our abilities we convince others of our great ability. Conversely, when we show up doubting ourselves, we convince others of our inability.

Do you know when you do which? If we continue to operate on auto pilot, we likely are not aware as often as could be. And if living our best life – however it is defined – is a goal, certainly communicating as your best self, is worth the time to read this book.

Learning how to communicate intentionally helps women to show up as their best version of herself. How would you like to more confidently set boundaries? Self-advocate? Speak up with self-assuredness? Increase your influence? Personally, or professionally there are countless interactions where others are assessing you; in mere seconds, others determine whether or not to believe you, trust you, follow you or respect you, whether you know it or not. Often, presenting ourselves with confidence increases our breadth of influence. Self-confidence is linked to almost every element involved in a happy and fulfilling life.[21] When we feel self-assured we show up differently.

Just in case you are thinking about confidence as boisterous, have you noticed I have yet to define confidence as loud, outgoing or charismatic? I know many quiet individuals who command attention, inspire and influence others without drawing attention to themselves in a loud and obnoxious manner. Confidence inspires and attracts, regardless if you are an extrovert, introvert or a little bit of both.

A perceived lack of confidence is likely costing you opportunities, fulfillment, and money.

When we feel confident and powerful, we walk a bit taller. We speak firmer. We experience more peace as we tend to focus more on our feelings about our ability and less about other's opinions. We take up more space. Our world needs more women to expand in to their best version of herself. What is stopping you? What would showing up with self-assuredness in any given situation, professional or personal, do in your life? How much stress would you avoid by believing in yourself and your ability, no matter the situation? Maneuvering life with a healthy dose of confidence will only open more doors of opportunity; the opportunity to think as the best of version of yourself, to honestly believe that you are worthy, valuable, capable and kind of freaking awesome!

This is not to say that you believe yourself to be perfect. (Don't get me started on the perfection myth as this unrealistic ideal that is detrimental to our mental /emotional health.) Quite the contrary... confidence is that you believe yourself to be capable and worthy, *despite* any shortcomings. This quest for perfectionism is quite the confidence killer. Think of a time when you felt very self-conscious or had any degree of self-doubt. What was the situation? Who else was involved? What were the causes of yourself doubt? Now, think of a time when you felt very self-assured. Likely you felt strong, knowledgeable, attractive and/or even powerful. Recall the situation and the source/s of this confidence. If you had the choice, who would not want to feel more self-assured in such a situation? Now imagine if you could present yourself this confidently more often than not, regardless of how much confidence you are actually experiencing.

One major part of exuding confidence and influencing others is how you show up to others which has a lot to do with body language or non-verbal language. Do you know what messages your body language might be sending? Take inventory. Be aware of your body position, movement, facial expressions and how much space you take up! Point blank: Do you *look* confident?

WHY IT MATTERS.

If you feel confident, you communicate from a self-assured standpoint. And others can perceive this confidence. If you feel self-conscious or experience major self-doubt, you also bring this to each communication situation. Who would you put your trust in, someone with self-belief or self-doubt? Now, with an increased awareness and a little adjustment of our body language and word choices, we are ready to implement the simple hacks to present yourself as your best self; a self-assured individual who inspires trust and respect of others. Then, watch opportunities swing your way.

Confidence empowers.

Confidence inspires.

Confidence influences.

Confidence is communicated through your expressive behaviors.

ACTION ITEMS:

1. Go to a mirror. Impersonate someone who is very nervous, with a high level of self-doubt. Take stock of your facial expression, your shoulders, posture, stance. Now, switch these expressive behaviors to a confident persona. Note the differences.

2. Identify the next communication situation where you want to come off confidently (even if you do not feel confident at the

time). What might your body need to be doing to show confidence, authenticity and self-belief?

CHAPTER 4:
TAKE UP SPACE

Loras College Admission staff *(Go Duhawks!)* were training a group of student workers in 1995, on how to take prospective students on a campus tour. Walking backwards while talking to a visiting group was a point of particular interest. As awkward as it sounded, their point was to never turn your back on the group you were touring, aka, your audience. The most important lesson I learned that semester came when we entered the weight room and it had nothing to do with physical fitness.

The student-tour-guides-in-training approached the entrance door to the weight room. The staff person stopped us all, looked at the group of four of us straight in the eyes, lowered the tone of his voice and said, "When you are touring a prospective student, you do not hesitate here. You enter this weight room walking them all the way to the back wall, explaining what the weight room offers to all students. Do this especially when you are touring a female student. You must *show* them that they belong in this weight room. This facility is not just for male athletes. You must show them by your action that they can take up space here, no matter how many people are in here at the time. Our female prospects must feel the space that is rightfully theirs." This may not be earth shattering now, but back in

1995, when male sports teams were the pride and joy of college athletics, regardless of their actual record, this was a momentous lesson for a female student at the time.

I have never forgotten this experience. In fact, I have often thought of that training, even now, when I need a reminder myself, or when I am working with clients who struggle with taking up the space. In fact, most recently, while I was at the YMCA in the weights area, there was a man, spreading out while bouncing between three different weight stations .His belongings were draped over the three machines. (#eyeroll) My lesson at the Loras weight room came flooding back. While my first tendency was to head to a different machine, I remembered, that I too, have every right to take up space here. I had an equal right to at least one of those machines he could not possibly use all at the same time. I respectfully but notably claimed my physical space next to three-machine-man and got my full desired workout in that day. Taking up space does not only happen in weight rooms, of course. You can take up space in meeting rooms, breakout rooms, board rooms, court rooms and any room you can bring your value.

My clients have had to work on taking up more space on stage during their company-wide presentations, during staff meetings, negotiations, witness stands, and during difficult conversations. Do you claim your space? Do you ever find yourself shrinking, physically, when you are not sure of yourself? In meetings, virtual or in-person, how do you take up more space? Do you present yourself as if you know that you belong? That this is your space too? That you have equal right as anyone else to be present?

In various communication situations, women may cross our legs, keep our hands on our phone or clasped together, both which draw our limbs closer together, thus making us smaller.

When we take up less space, we feel less powerful.[22]

One of my clients was troubled because during a meeting with certain team members, she felt like her ideas were not being heard. She was feeling as if she was not being 'allowed' to contribute as other members on this team. We worked together on her preparation and one part of this was how she physically showed up to this team. I coached her on how to take up more physical and verbal space. When she walked into the next meeting, her posture was erect, she walked confidently into the room, made eye contact with attendees and verbally greeted the group. She then took a seat in the middle of the table where she could see everyone equally. She spread her notes, laptop and phone out instead of stacking them on top of each other. Her belongings were now taking up more space. She sat back with good posture, spread her shoulders out, laying her arms on the arm rests. She did not grab her phone as she usually did, while waiting of the meeting to begin. Instead she looked at the team members in the eye and participated in small talk with the rest of them. Her presence was noted. She did this every team meeting, each week. It took three weeks until she contributed an idea to which the committee agreed to implement.

Dr. Amy Cuddy is a social scientist whose first findings on power-posing and self-reported feelings caught my attention many years ago. A former student sent me her now famous, Ted Talk, "Your body language may shape who you are" that has garnered almost 70 million views at time of print. I followed her research and was interested to see backlash on her research on this topic of postural feedback. Then again, when a woman, a vetted expert in her field, accomplishes success and fame, is it really surprising the naysayers come out of the woodwork? If the topic of taking up more space to feel more powerful resonates with you, you will want to follow this story. If not, move ahead to the next section at your own disadvantage. A very long story quite short:

Dr. Amy Cuddy conducted research as a social psychologist. She was at Northwestern University and then a tenured position at Harvard University, teaching MBA students. At some point, fellow academics began to scrutinize research methods of various research projects in the social sciences. [23] Science methodology is important and this group of academic peers felt that subjectivity was running too rampant in certain published studies. When Dr. Cuddy's research was becoming more well received by the mass media, the scrutinizing academics decided to focus on Dr. Cuddy's research. Months and years follow. Her fellow researches also get a piece of the action in challenging her.[24]

As I followed this unfortunate saga over the last few years, I have come to realize that at times, as a woman, we take up plenty of space and it makes others uncomfortable. They may come for us and we may face backlash. I have not cracked the code on how to unequivocally avoid such scrutiny but I do know our job is simply to do our best, be prepared but do not shrink and allow others to take up our space. I have already received criticism about this book and it is not even published yet as I write this. But do you think I'll let that stop me from moving this book forward? Not a chance.

While Dr. Amy Cuddy is no longer teaching and has left Harvard, she is still writing, publishing, speaking and stands by her research that power posing does indeed make an individual feel more powerful. She is a successful professional speaker, and her book, " Presence: Bringing Your Boldest Self to Your Biggest Challenges" is a New York Times, Washington Post, USA Today, Wall Street Journal, Publisher's Weekly, and Globe and Mail bestseller. It's been published in 35 languages and has sold more than half a million copies.[25] One might say this is a great example of taking up space, despite making others uncomfortable.

Do your best. Be Prepared.
Claim your space that is rightfully yours. Do not shrink.

Now, when I talk about taking up your physical space, am I asking you to manspread? Absolutely not. However, might there be a middle ground? Let's first talk about the physical space before we talk about verbal space.

HOW TO TAKE UP PHYSICAL SPACE

1. **Breathe:** The first key to taking up more physical space is to breathe. As we will find when we talk in a subsequent chapter about combatting any nerves, breathing to speak and interact with others, is quite different than breathing to simply live. Diaphragmatic breathing is the best way to expand your lungs and get the necessary oxygen to your brain which controls much of our behaviors in any given communication situation. When you breathe, you expand your belly not your shoulders. Your waistband should move. Start with breathing. The benefits are numerous but for now, anytime you can expand any part of your body, is a win. A double win if it also helps you to think more clearly and decrease any feelings of nervousness or anxiety.

2. **Take Inventory:** Since most of our workday is spent in some form of communication, we often rely on auto-pilot during communication situations. However, I invite you become more aware of how you show up. Take a physical inventory as if you have a camera focused on your body.

   - **Chin:** Start with the top of your body, your head. Individuals who feel powerful, generally, communicate this with a chin that is elevated. Think of Olympic athletes who win – look at their winning position. Track and field, gymnastics, hockey, curling (yes, I am not sure why curling is an Olympic sport either, but here we are) when victorious athletes' chins are not sunken, pointing down. This feeling of power is often shown by a raised chin. This is likely where the phrase, 'keep your chin up' originates. Don't be sad or down, keep that chin up and feel good! If you are constantly looking down at a phone, your chin is pointed down. Stop doing that.

- **Shoulders:** Become aware of your shoulders. Are they in a relaxed or slouched position? This may communicate a lack of confidence, competence or enthusiasm. Your posture should be erect as possible without looking awkward. Practice erect posture and what it looks like on you. This is why I like wearing heels, which my chiropractor continues to lecture me on, because the heel forces me to throw my shoulders back in a more confident position. Find the sweet spot for yourself. What erect posture feels comfortable to you and doable? People will sniff out inauthentic behaviors so it is imperative that you find a confident posture that you can adapt as your own. I encourage you to simply not default to a slouched version of yourself. This can easily communicate a lack of confidence.

- **Limbs:** Where are your limbs as you sit or stand? This is equally important in video and face-to-face meetings. Using your hands and arms for natural gesturing when you speak can increase your credibility. When your body language is congruent with your content, people believe what you say more than if these behaviors are incongruent. When you are taking up space, your limbs should be comfortably as far apart as possible. Now, we must be a bit careful on the legs here as there are some signs we likely do *not* want to send. This is not a racy *Fatal Attraction* scene, after all! (If the movie title does not ring a bell Google it, you'll get it.) What I suggest is to not always default to crossing your legs if you don't need to. Of course, this may depend what items of clothing we wear as I will always cross legs in a dress or skirt.

However, I am then sure to expand my arms and shoulders as much as I can. At times, when wearing pants, I will sit with a more expansive position. I am *not* taking about manspreading with legs wide apart or one leg on a knee. My point here is to remind you to take inventory. What *are* your legs doing? Where are your arms by default?

3. **Be Intentional:** Too often, we assume a physical position by default and we do not intentionally think about our body position. I am asking you to think intentionally about how you present yourself, physically, and how you can take up more space at any given moment. When in the office, out with a client, how do you walk, approach others or present yourself, physically? Do not default to your comfort zone, as easy as it may be.

Taking up more physical space is great when you are physically in front of someone, online or face to-face. However, how can we show up verbally? Taking up more space verbally is similar. Think of how to get your voice heard in any given communication situation. Too often, I have heard women state that in meetings, it can become too challenging to contribute. Either too many people are speaking or they have a moment where they doubt themselves and believe they have nothing valuable to contribute. Clearly there will be times where it may be best to stay quiet. However, never should you stay quiet if it is *only* because it is too much work to speak up.

Taking up verbal space also has three steps.

HOW TO TAKE UP VERBAL SPACE

1. **Prepare:** When you desire to take up space in a communication situation, always prepare. This does not mean you must spend hours upon hours reading up on phrases or rehearsing how you are going to say

something (although those items do help). It may simply be a brief you need to review to be well-read on documents. Prepare by reviewing any documentation that may be involved in the conversation. Then, survey the social context. Could there be a difficult conversation ahead of you? Play it out and identify how you may react, if you were communicating as the best version of yourself. Often, I will jot down a phrase/statement on a post it note next to my laptop so if I need the phrase, I am ready. How can you best prepare for the virtual situation?

2. **Set Goals:** In a moment of proactivity, ahead of this situation, ask yourself how you'd like to contribute. Do you want to ask a question? Provide an idea? Offer an objection to a suggestion? Provide an alternative solution? Align yourself with a specific person? What is important to note here is that I am not suggesting you talk just to talk. Setting a goal of how you'd like to contribute gives you a target. It also forces you to prioritize. Of course, you can always offer an opinion but when you have thoughtfully designed a goal and prepared, you are then deliberate in your communication actions. Thus, appearing prepared, confident and competent.

3. **Seek a partner:** At times, we may see a difficult conversation or difference of opinion coming. When possible, I suggest having a proactive conversation with an ally. Give them a heads up on what you are thinking about and communicate that you would appreciate their support. This may look very different and of course depends on what the situation actually entails.

For example, I was in a high-level task force meeting with an organization's board of directors. I was the least experienced attendee; however, I had done my due diligence and knew a specific concern of the organization's president (due to a question I asked him in a previous meeting). Before the meeting, I texted an ally and mentioned what I was going to suggest. This "friendly" agreed it was a good idea to bring up this specific subject and he'd support me. When it came time for my concern to get brought up, a response by a senior board member surprisingly (or not) tried to squash this concern. As he was ending his reasoning on why my suggestion should not be considered, my ally jumped in (which was appropriate at the time) to further support my idea, he then asked me for clarification. I was then able to expand on why I believe this was the right move. It took some time but months later, my idea was presented to the President from this task force and was approved. Could I have done this all by myself? Sure, maybe. But with the contribution of my ally, it only amplified my idea so I could later expand, thus assisting me in taking up more verbal space, intentionally. Have a proactive conversation with an ally, before you actually may need a little help.

Taking up intentional and deliberate verbal space is important for women. #takeupspace

While this is very different than talking just to talk, taking up this space is an opportunity to show how you are a prepared, intelligent and competent team member. It also reminds those in power that you, your expertise and contributions are valuable.

ACTION ITEMS:

1. Take inventory. What is your default physical body language? Where is your posture? Arms? Facial expressions? How do carry yourself around the office/into client offices/during meetings?

2. Practice. Practice in front of a mirror or record yourself assuming different iterations of your body language. How can you communicate support? Doubt? Approval? Disapproval with your physical expressions?

CHAPTER 5:

BOUNDARIES.
SET THEM.
KEEP THEM.
COMMUNICATE THEM.

Even if you are not a dog person, envision two different people walking their own dogs. Person A has a dog that is walking in sync with its owner, at the right pace and there is no friction on the dog's collar around its neck. They both seem to be headed in the same direction the entire walk. When Person A commands the dog to stop before crossing the street, the dog pauses, before they resume their walk safely.

Person B has a dog that is running any direction where it can smell the scent of a squirrel. The owner is trying to keep up, following the dog in each direction. The dog leash expands then snaps in friction while yanking the dog back or the owner forward. Person B walks straight for a bit, but is then pulled in a different direction. This goes on for the duration of the walk. The owner is frustrated from their walk and does not seem to know why their dog won't ever walk on a leash well.

While I am no dog trainer, it is obvious that Person A has better control. They have set boundaries for their dog and has likely had to train the dog on who is in charge. Person B might be doing their best, trying to let the dog have a fun walk, but in the meantime, the dog is out of control. Dog B does not know of any boundaries other than feeling the yank of their neck when the leash runs out. This process exhausts Person B, they feel out of control and hopeless. Person B is at the mercy of a dog and lets the dog have control. And while I am not the famous dog trainer, Cesar Millan, I know this is not productive nor effective.

This dog walking example is similar to how we must view the process of setting boundaries. Who do you want to be in control of what you are willing or not willing to do? Your supervisor? That manipulative friend whom you half love and half loathe? That overzealous neighbor? Your colleagues? Your Catholic/Jewish (insert any adjective) – guilt – loving Mom? The group in your social circle? In the everyday happenstance of fielding requests, our boundaries are in flux. The bottom line however, is that you are in control of what you choose to do or not do. Too often we forget this notion and we wait to see what direction someone will pull us. Yet, in that moment, we may find that that we are not prepared and we do not know how to say no without feeling badly so say yes solely by default. Then we get tired, frustrated and even angry at those responsible as if it is their fault. We are the ones who have control over our decisions. Of course, not all these decisions are going to be obvious or easy but I must remind you that only *you* are in control of your boundaries. We just need the tools to communicate our desire to not offend others while also making our boundaries known. The answer may just be in the difference of purpose on how men and women communicate.

Women generally communicate with peripheral goals to connect with others in a social and supportive manner. Conversely, men tend to communicate to solve a problem and complete a task.[26] It is said that women engage in "rapport" talk while men engage in "report" talk. This difference between genders, at times, can pose quite a challenge for women. How do we set boundaries yet cultivate connection to others? How do we say 'no' and maintain social support of those we just rejected? How do we decline an invitation without feeling as if it is a show of no interest in that person? If women communicate in a manner that establishes rapport or good will, it can feel uncomfortable to set boundaries for fear of offending others. Possibly to help us communicate our boundaries we just need to reframe how we view communicating our desired boundaries?

What if setting boundaries is a promise to ourselves to honor our goals, desires and capabilities? #boundariespromise

The biggest reason I see that women say yes, when they want to say no, is the lack of knowledge on how to say no. "I did not know what to say, so I just said yes, that I would take on that project though I do not have the time." What would it look like if you knew how to set boundaries that you were proud of and without sounding offensive or rude? What I find most interesting is that many women put the needs of others before their own in these types of situations because they think it is easier. They may find it easier to take on more work or be uncomfortable than to self-advocate, though this is not a mutually exclusive option.

What is the answer? Setting boundaries, the healthy way! This chapter is not going to focus on *what* boundaries you must set but will provide tools on *how* to communicate while setting those boundaries.

- Have you ever been asked by family members to attend a family celebration that you sincerely did not want to or could not make?

- Have you been asked by a friend to go along with a plan with which you were not comfortable?

- Have you ever felt guilted in to participating in something you did not feel was right?

- Have you ever said 'yes' to a supervisor or colleague when you really wanted to say 'no'?

- Have you ever not spoken up because you did not want to be perceived as a bitch?

One sign that you can improve how you communicate your boundaries is guilt.

When my husband and I started having children, the words "Mom Guilt" ran around in the circles of my life. Friends who had paying jobs felt guilt for leaving their children at home. Friends who were home with kids all day felt guilt when their impatience bubbled up because they needed a break from wiping noses and butts! They also felt guilty at times because they were not financially contributing to their household. This type of guilt led to a lot of iffy decision making, at the time, for many of us.

A client fell into a habit of getting stuck with her officemate's work. She said "They always make a case, in the moment, of why I should be in charge of their pile of paperwork. I felt the guilt of not looking like a team player, so it is just easier to take the work on, rather than argue with them." We worked to increase her understanding of the fact that there are more than two options than saying yes or engaging in an unpleasant conversation all based on a feeling of guilt. We worked through realistic scenarios and she developed a few sayings that she felt was respectful but also empowered to set her boundaries. Her officemate eventually took the clue and no longer asked her to accept the extra work. And bonus, the client built confidence each time she experienced this scenario which only strengthened her boundary-setting skills.

Too often, we use guilt as an excuse to say 'yes' when we really don't want to. Have you ever said or heard, "I said yes because I just felt guilty."? When you do this, you deprioritize your own value. You, in essence, are saying "What you want is more important than what I want or feel is right." A phrase that a former First Lady, Eleanor Roosevelt, is credited to inspiring, is "No one can make you feel anything, without your permission."

No one can make us feel anything without our permission. #noguiltwithoutpermission

The story goes that in 1935 the Secretary of Labor was invited to be a speaker at the University of California Berkeley on the Charter Day of the school. The host, at the time, felt that there should not have been be a politician as a speaker so the host refused to serve out their duties at that event.

Later at the White House press event, the First Lady was asked if she felt the Secretary was 'snubbed' and she replied, "A snub is the effort of a person who feels superior to make someone else feel inferior." She made clear she didn't think the labor secretary fell within the category of the 'snubable.' [27]

The labor secretary was not snubable, according to the First Lady. Are you snubable? Do others 'make' you feel inferior? And if so, why? How? Since we know that our true feelings and attitudes leak out of us, might we be carrying the look of someone who is snubable into every interaction? What does snubable look like? Snubable may appear like someone who is unsure of themselves. Someone who does not do what they actually want to, instead they agree because it is easier and more comfortable at the time. There are people who prey on snubable souls. Don't be one of them. Why do we allow others to make us feel anything? I do understand that it is our human nature to want justice and what is 'right' to be accomplished. I understand why it is when we see an injured animal, we feel compassion. This, though, is *not* what I am talking about. I am talking about giving up your power in a situation where others may feel that they have power over you and your boundaries. Hopefully you recall my statement earlier that only *you* are in control of your boundaries.

Any time you say yes *only* due to guilt, you are giving away permission like roses on Valentine's Day. The best way to avoid this is to know, proactively, what you are willing and not willing to do. Then, come up with a phrase (out of your communication toolbox, discussed soon) that you are comfortable with, and use that phrase as a response to the request. It may sound like:

- Would love to; just can't this time.

- No, I can't.

- Thank you for thinking of me, I just can't make it work right now.

- That sounds fun – unfortunately it won't be possible this time.

- I am honored you'd ask me, although I cannot do this, how about I help you find someone?

- Thanks for asking me, I just can't – but can I ask around to see if anyone else may be the right fit?

While these specific phrases may not work for your particular situation, you can make a list of phrases that you are comfortable with that will help you to communicate your 'no'. Please note, I am advocating that you say no to any suggestion, demand or invitation where you know deep down you'd prefer to say no and/or *should* say no. Again, I am not telling you what boundaries to set, moreover, I'm suggesting *how* to communicate these boundaries.

I was sitting on a pool-side chair on my family's spring vacation a few years ago, after a particularly busy season. After a winter in the Chicagoland area, some warm sun was just what I needed. My husband and I both love the seven days in the spring we take to soak up Vitamin D from the sunny beach side. We are not adventurers on vacation usually. Particularly this annual tradition, we sit on pool chairs for seven days, as long as the weather allows us. This vacation, my in-laws were with us, which is always fun to have multiple generations relax and enjoy each other. In her generous way, my mother-in-law, invited my daughter to go shopping one day. They invited me as well, since all the females of the family were going shopping. I politely declined but my mother-in-law asked again. I know she was thinking how nice it would be to have her mother, her daughter-in-law and her granddaughter, four generations, share a fun day of shopping together. The only problem was that I was *really* enjoying relaxing with my husband (her son) pool side. The weather was my favorite, sunny and 80 degrees. I did not want to go anywhere. For the second time, I politely explained I get seven days all year to enjoy this weather, next to a pool and as much fun as shopping would be, I really wanted to relax. She took it in good stride and understood my desire to stay back. All the ladies had a fabulous time and we were able to look at all their fun treasures when they returned hours later, to the same pool chair I was on when they left.

I could have let some guilt creep in as I fully understood the desire my mother-in-law had. She is very thoughtful so she likely did not want to exclude me. However, my family has a busy schedule all year, especially in the spring months. My husband and I look at this vacation as our only restful time before an avalanche of spring sporting events and a seven-days-a-week schedule of kid activities. The bottom line was that I wanted to do what I knew would allow me to relax, recharge and stay centered so I could show up fully for myself and my family. It may seem silly to you as you read this but I knew deep down that shopping was the last thing I wanted to do in that moment. Luckily, I have an understanding and non-judgmental mother-in-law. :-) Believe me, I was not moving from that pool chair, that day.

When was the last time you said 'yes' but really wanted to say 'no'? No seriously, take a moment to contemplate.

- What was that situation?

- How long ago was it?

- What was asked of you?

- Why did you want to say no?

- Did you feel like you had a 'right' so say no?

At times, we weigh our options. We come up with great excuses as to why we should probably just say yes. Then, at some point in the future, we dread having to make good on our agreement and wonder why we did indeed agree to this ask of us.

Next time you are in this situation I'd suggest you consider the following three prompts as you determine your boundaries:

1. What does your gut tell you to do? Try not to second guess yourself. Discern the motivation behind your gut feeling. Don't make up excuses to doubt yourself. You are a grown-ass woman, trust yourself.

For example, I had to say no to a wonderful invitation to head out to dinner with friends recently. Now, I love me some friends and always have a good time. However, that time period fell smack in the middle of two weeks where I was busy and gone most evenings. I yearned for one night at home with my family. I needed a family dinner in pajamas, a relaxing evening at home to recharge with my family. Luckily, I have reasonable friends who understood why I had to say no at that time. I then volunteered to set up the next time we are all out so there was security around the fact that there *would* be a next time.

2. Find the words. You will read in the Communication Tool Box Chapter, you should always have phrases that you are comfortable saying, at the ready. When the phrases are already in your head, you don't have to spend time worrying about if you should say something or what you should actually say. Find the words

on how you can say 'no thank you'. Start a journal, a Notes page in your phone and keep track of phrases on how to communicate 'no' in a way which you are comfortable.

3. Anticipate and practice. Anticipate the people or requests of you, that are coming down the pipeline. When you see that family member, do they always ask you to do something you have no interest in? That friend who always asks for the favor that you dread? Anticipate who may be asking what from you. Then, select the phrase of which you feel most comfortable and practice saying it.

Bottom line: You get to decide what you are willing to do. You do not have to explain an elaborate story on all of your feelings. You can easily smile and say, "Thank you, that sounds like it could be fun/worthwhile/interesting, but I just cannot."

Know Your Boundaries. State Them. Believe them. Own them.

ACTION ITEMS:

1. Say what you mean. Don't say 'yes' if you feel 'no'.

2. Don't second guess yourself. You are a free willing, human being. Your time and thoughts are valuable and you get to decide what you want or do not want to do.

3. Just say no. Find the phrases you are most comfortable with. Provide an alternative if you'd like. Say no if you are feeling no. There is a reason. Trust yourself.

CHAPTER 6:
BIG GIRL PANTS PRESENTATION SKILLS: PART 1

-THE WHY-

Too often, I hear a woman comment to me how they could never stand up in front of audiences and publicly present. They joke that they try to avoid any occasion of public speaking as much as they can in their current role. However, I ask anyone who can relate, to view speaking in front of others, a bit differently. If you have ever had to negotiate a salary, persuade a child in some manner, or participate in a job interview, you have publicly spoken. Public speaking is just that, communicating your thoughts to others. One major element of showing up as the best version of yourself, with your big girl pants on, is delivering presentations, both informally and formally. Even if you may think this chapter may not apply to you, I assure you that anyone can benefit from an increased skillset in sharing your thoughts with others. If you can do this effectively as the best version of yourself, what opportunities may lie ahead of you that you had not previously considered? This chapter will give you tips to gain the right mindset to increase your confidence in delivering a presentation, putting your best foot forward.

Instead of dreading public speaking, think of it as a way to showcase your brilliance and unique contributions. #publicspeakingisexciting #biggirlpants

Whether you find yourself avoiding a speaking situation regularly or you speak in formal presentations so often that you don't think much about it, or you avoid the near occasion, (and everything in between) I promise you likely have not considered the common landmines that curb your potential. These obstacles can be dangerous and become quite detrimental to your success. Clients tell me about their experiences that usually fall into one of three categories:

- My job does not necessitate many public speaking opportunities, so I'm good!

- Oh, I speak all the time and have no problem talking to others.

- No. Nope. No Way. I avoid speaking at all costs. Hell no!

At first you may think these three scenarios do not have much in common however, the bottom line is wherever your self-confidence lies in delivering presentations there is *always* a new opportunity to take control of how you can communicate as the best version of yourself. When you avoid presentations or take them for granted you are not performing at your best. You may be allowing fear to dictate your path, stunting your growth and potential.

It is time to take control, become intentional and ensure that you no longer have to avoid public speaking or take it for granted. You will begin to gain new confidence and even level up your ability when it comes to presenting your ideas in front of others with a few unique strategies. But first, it is important to understand why it is so important for women to equip themselves with the ability to present confidently. Plenty of communication, business and leadership experts have plenty to say about a woman's ability to deliver a presentation. The importance of public speaking is agreed upon by most success experts and here are two of my favorite perspectives:

"While women have advanced in many arenas, women will never achieve their full potential if they avoid public speaking." [28]

"...if you can present well, others will think of you as a capable, articulate individual. The ability to speak, present and facilitate groups is the number one skill for women in business today."[29]

The problem? Too often women underestimate the power of their presentation skills. Often, when we hear the term "present" or "public speaking" we may immediately think about our favorite executive or team leader that seems to have a natural ability to present. Subsequently, we then compare our ability against their ability. And in our minds, we lose because we cannot compete with someone with such 'natural ability'. However, this common scenario is not accurate and is only feeding your fear. Stop that. Let's refine your thinking about anytime you have the opportunity to share your thoughts and ideas in front of others. You have original and valuable thoughts to share. And, I would argue you can communicate these thoughts in a manner that will genuinely help others, once they hear you in an effective manner.

Often, we hear a reason why women are uncomfortable with public speaking is a lack of experience and/or confidence. Boosting confidence on how to structure and deliver a presentation might be all you need at this point. You cannot show up as the best version of yourself if you do not show up at all. Showing up really is most of the battle. Starting today, don't avoid the occasions where you can showcase your brilliance, your thoughts, ideas and perspective. Letting fear of any public speaking prevent you from growing into your best version of yourself is hurting you and curbing your success. What might it feel like to no longer dread public speaking? How might your mindset or professional life change if you became *great* at speaking in front of others?

Think about when you have heard a great presentation. Often, when we are enjoying a presentation, it may look too easy and quite natural to the speaker. As mentioned previously, we chalk it up to the presenter's natural ability and therefore internalize the fact that we may lack that ability. This is our first misstep. Speaking in front of others is a skill that must be learned, practiced and honed. Congrats, this is a step along your journey claiming your confidence and competence by improving your speaking skills! While is it true, that some individuals have a more natural ability, presenting in front of others is a muscle that can absolutely be built. You do not have to feel stuck in cringe mode each time you have the opportunity to present yourself to others. Below are a few guidelines before we dive into the actual steps to a glorious presentation in the subsequent chapter.

GUIDELINES: YOUR *BIG GIRL PANTS* PRESENTATION SKILLS

Have you ever sat through a meeting that should have been an email? When meetings are not effective, most blame can be placed on how meetings are facilitated and how the information is presented. Whether you avoid the opportunity to present or facilitate or you do it so often you operate on auto pilot, I suggest you rethink how you approach the sharing of your information by focusing on the following considerations to confidently present.

1. Name the Inner Critic – then show her the door!

No matter what your true feelings are about delivering presentations, we all have an inner critic whose voice tends to rise when we find ourselves confronted with the occasion of speaking in front of others. No matter where you are on the love (or hatred) public speaking continuum, you will likely hear an inner whisper that reminds you not to screw up, that you are going to make a fool of yourself, or encourages you to play it safe, or that it really does not matter. *Do not listen!* Instead...

Identify that inner critic voice. Name your inner critic and tell her to shut up and show her the door to exit your brain. I name my inner critic, Peg. She sucks. Peg likes to tell me that I cannot possibly write a book, that I don't have enough experience, focus or capacity. I like to shut Peg down with facts, i.e., I have plenty of experience in writing, I can and have focused and can always manage my capacity as I have already proven. I encourage you to do the same. Maybe you don't have a ton of experience speaking in front of others, tell your Peg that you don't need it, that you have plenty of real experience and know how communicate the necessary content. Possibly your Peg tells you that it doesn't really matter and no one is going to pay attention, so you'll just wing it and hope for the best. Tell your Peg that you will not be derailed from communicating as your best self. Period.

Of course, it is natural to feel anxiety or doubt at times in our own ability. What is not healthy however, is to acquiesce to the inner critic and stay in that space. When we analyze our strengths and areas of improvement, we evolve and improve and grow. However, keep things in perspective when you are about to speak. Shut that inner critic's voice up quickly with facts. Rely on facts not feelings.

Rely on facts not feelings. #factsnotfeelings

Remind yourself of the facts of your experience, position, situation where you were put in a position to present so you can and will show up as the best version of yourself. Tell your Peg to sit down and shut up.

2. Do not Underestimate the Benefit of Breathing

It sounds way too elementary that most of us simply forget to breathe. Remember, breathing to sustain life is very different than breathing to speak in front of an audience. While we must all breathe, the manner in which we do it varies greatly. When we present in front of others it is very likely that our adrenaline spikes and we may experience a surge of nervous energy. Butterflies in your stomach, shaky hands or voice, an increased rate of speech are just a few examples of how you may experience nervousness. Breathing is the quickest way to combat your nerves. Your diaphragm (think area behind your waistband) should expand when you breathe correctly in this case. Your waistband not your shoulders, should move. This allows the flow of oxygen to hit your brain and works to calm nerves, letting your brain concentrate on what it needs to do.

A study conducted amid communication students in higher education found that breathing has profound effects on the sympathetic and parasympathetic nervous systems. Think, heart rate, perspiration, muscle tension, rapid or shallow breathing. The level of stress in any given situation influences the degree of the reaction.[30] The problem is that this tactic can be viewed as way too simple and many presenters forget all about breathing. This is why we may hear our voice shake or we feel out of breath for no apparent reason. Diaphragmatic breathing has been proven to decrease feelings of nervousness and help combat adrenaline spikes. When you breathe appropriately you allow more oxygen flow to your brain and extremities. When any level of communication anxiety presents, intentional and specific breathing exercises will only help decrease nerves and calm any physical reactions which may distract from your actual presentation. This deep breathing strategy has helped to reduce test anxiety, lower blood pressure, lower asthmatic and breathlessness symptoms, lessen anxiety and panic attacks, lower epilepsy episodes, reduce change of a second coronary heart attack and even showed a trend toward decreased anxiety with dental patients.[31] Simply put, breathing is where it's at!

3. Do Not Wing It.

You may have a handle of specific content however, do you know what this 'audition' can do for you as far as social perceptions? What if this triggers, unknowingly, a thought in someone's head about how competent you are and sets into motion, a great opportunity for you in the coming months or even years? Prepare as if you are in an audition. You can come across naturally and authentically while still being prepared.

I was facilitating a program at a volunteer event. I prepared my notes so I'd be able to present authentically and confidently. Notice this was a volunteer position and I was not being paid to facilitate. I could have easily thought "no need to prepare, I am working for free and no potential clients are in the audience." However, I believe anytime I am in front of others, it is important for me to stay authentic and be prepared. In fact, being prepared allows me to be authentic as I present. The event went well and I thought nothing of it, until a few weeks later. I received an email from someone in attendance who asked me to present for their global company women's leadership group. This was an absolute ideal client for me that I never saw coming. I was hired and had an amazing experience with this group that I likely never would have, had I not been fully prepared. You never know. I could not have anticipated that awesome opportunity. You may never know what opportunities you don't earn because you are not prepared for that meeting facilitation or speech presentation or worse, you decline the invitation to share your ideas with others.

The next chapter will explore the how-to behind presentation preparation. This chapter calls upon you to fully understand the why of being prepared and taking any speaking opportunity seriously.

ACTION ITEMS:

1. Practice quality breathing throughout your day. Deep breath, expanding your waistband. Try a breathing app. My favorite, at time of writing, is the Breathing App which signals specific time periods of inhaling and exhaling. Work on breathing to combat nerves, as a regular habit.

2. Keep your radar up on speaking opportunities and what your initial reaction is to them. Consider rephrasing your reaction in your head to "... that would be exciting" instead of any negative self-talk. Note if your attitude may begin to change regarding speaking opportunities.

BIG GIRL PANTS PRESENTATION SKILLS: PART 2

- THE HOW TO'S -

Once we have become more intentional about how we approach the idea of presenting in front of others, it is time to gain confidence and skill level. How do I effectively present in front of others? What is appropriate? What is effective? And what will lead me to a successful presentation? This chapter will give you step-by-step instructions that you can reference as a quick guide at any time, not just when you are reading the entirety of this book. Fold this page (or bookmark it for those of you perfectionists) and know you can come back here anytime you are called upon to present in front of others!

THE DO'S OF A CONFIDENT 'BIG GIRL PANTS' PRESENTATION -

1. **What is the Purpose?** First, identify the purpose of this presentation. Know the overall goal. Identifying the purpose of your presentation will likely cut your prep time. Set the foundation with articulating your purpose. Would you like to:

   - Inform your team of current numbers?

   - Provide a status report?

   - Persuade your executive team that you must hire additional staff?

   - Campaign for a raise?

   - Introduce a new concept?

   - Pitch a new idea?

This foundational purpose is not something that needs to be stated out loud but should be developed to have a clear purpose laid out before you begin. You cannot know the path if you do not know where you are headed. As the speaker it is your job to guide your audience down the right path of communication. What are you communicating? What is the purpose? If nothing else, be able to finish the following sentence: "The purpose of today's presentation is to...."

It is all too easy to skip this foundational step. However, you will lose an audience as quickly as they enter the meeting room, if you are not clear on your foundational purpose of your presentation. And if the purpose of your presentation could be better communicated in an email, contact me, we have some work to do together. :-) (No, seriously, meg@megbucaro. com)

2. **Own your Content.** Do you know exactly what you will be presenting? Do the work. Compile the data, survey the participants, conduct the research. Organize the flow. Briefly outline the key ideas of your content. Visualize the presentation aids. There is plenty of pre-work. Manage your time so 'running out of time' is no excuse. In fact, I find that it is often the case that it is not that we don't want to do well, we just don't have enough time to thoroughly prepare. At the end of this chapter, you will see a short list of simple hacks to improve your presentation skills in case of urgency! Plan accordingly to know your content.

Years ago, I worked with a team of sales people within an organization. As part of their training, I observed all of their initial sales presentations. At some point, they all stumbled over a few slides and many of them read from slides. After a little digging I realized they were handed a slide deck from another department responsible for brand management. While I understood the benefit on staying uniformly on brand, this team never felt like they owned some parts of the information they had to present, therefore the flow of information was not smooth. I believe this cost them business.

Knowing your content goes beyond understanding the words on a slide. Own the concepts, the flow of information, the transitions. Be keenly aware of where the presentation is heading at all times. Work it, rework it until it makes sense to you and you feel that you own the content. Make it your own.

3. **Have Fun.** Delivering a presentation as if you are having fun does not mean you need to be jovial or smiling the entire time. This does mean that you should be able to deliver in a relaxed and confident manner. The goal is be comfortable in your own skin. When you are able to do this, even if the words do not come out perfectly, you do not appear uncomfortably nervous or unsure of yourself. When you are having

fun, you don't fixate on the tiniest details of self-consciousness. You can be yourself and let things flow. This is what delivering as if you are having fun means. In order to do this please explore your answer to the following questions:

- What would being comfortable in your own skin while presenting feel like for you?

- What would this look like?

- What would have to happen for you to feel this comfortable?

4. **Eye Contact:** Have notes or slides but do *not* read from these aids. You should have a brief set of notes to keep you on track, on time and focused. However, eye contact with a more extemporaneous delivery is best. Audience members tend to trust the speaker and lend them more credibility when there is a significant amount of eye contact and natural gesturing. This is why the extemporaneous delivery is so commonly practiced, desired and appreciated. When we read most of our presentation, we likely communicate a few different scenarios, all of which are negative:

1. I do not know my content well so I need to read.

2. You are not important enough for me to fully prepare and maintain good eye contact with you.

3. I am so nervous that I can't look at you so although I know my content I am not comfortable.

None of these scenarios are acceptable. All of these situations can be avoided. Delivery is often an element of a presentation that most people leave to chance. This is also the reason why so many presentations are boring or simply ineffective. Do *not* wing it, do not leave your delivery to chance. When conducting research about the differences between males and females it came down to the communication of confidence is lacking in females. What is funny is that when it came to presenting a speech, female college students reported that they felt more confident in their ability to deliver the speech, than their male counterparts. However, they presented less confidently. So, they felt more confident but showed up less confidently. What is the catch? Body Language. [32]

5. **Make your body language work for you:** How we communicate our confidence has everything to do with our body language or our nonverbal skills. While thousands of resources are available specifically on body language, let's focus on body language in the context of wanting to show up confidently while we present. After you know your content and have prepared and practiced, now it is time to plan your next move, literally. Ask yourself the following questions:

    - How will your body move throughout your presentation? (Especially when on Zoom.)

    - How much space will you have to move, in front of your audience?

    - Will you be sitting? Standing?

    - Is this a virtual presentation or an in person one?

    - What kind of energy do you need to bring to this presentation?

    - How do you want to show up? What are the adjectives that you hope your audience will use to describe you? Your presentation?

    - How can you make that happen?

Being intentional may make all the difference. If you are thinking you simply don't have time for all of this preparation, I assure you this does not take as long as you may think. I can answer the afore mentioned questions in mere seconds. Even if this took you five minutes to answer, wouldn't five minutes of this type of preparation be worth the investment into your success?

6. **Stay focused. Respect Other's Time.** Your listeners are giving you their time. Respect it and them. I attended a meeting of communication professors, where an agenda was distributed ahead of time. The leader of the meeting ran through a few items that took exactly two hours. That was how long the meeting was scheduled. At the two-hour mark, he moved on to another agenda item and said, "Ok, now onto the *real* reason we called this meeting." It took him two hours to get to the real point? The irony was not lost on me. And still, his time management was unacceptable. We all planned two hours of meeting time on our calendars. I had to leave, respectfully and missed the *real* reason we were all meeting. I expected more from a communication professional but why would we be any different? :-)

Think about how you feel about a meeting that runs over its scheduled time. This is nothing but a mismanagement of time and expectation. When you have the attention of an audience, stay on track. It is a sign of respect. It also shows that you know what you are doing and have control over your content. It is not humorous to abuse this rule, it is unacceptable. If you have trouble with keeping a group conversation on track, have phrases in your communication toolbox, like:

1. "That is a good point, I just want to make sure we are respectful of everyone's busy schedule and in an effort to end on time, we need to move on to... I am happy to chat with you after the meeting."

2. "These are all great points; however, we have come to the point in the meeting where we need to stay focused on _____. So, you and I can circle back on that."

3. "I am writing that down as something we will need to circle back to, to be respectful of everyone's time right now, let's move forward with _____."

You have now discovered few fundamental truths about what makes a good presentation and how to get there. Remember, never avoid an opportunity to show up in front of others to present, simply out of fear. When you do not show up at all, you cannot possibly show up well! If you fall into the category of dreading having to get up in front of others to present, you may find it is easier to learn how to present well and commit yourself to improvement so you do not have to avoid this situation any longer. And even if you do not avoid this situation, your public speaking skillset can always evolve and improve.

ACTION ITEMS

1. Schedule time on your calendar for preparation. It does not have to be hours upon hours, but start small and be realistic. Take the steps included in this book and make a 'Realistic Preparation Checklist" for yourself. What can you do to become more effective and confident in your presentation skills?

CHAPTER 7:
THE COMMUNICATION TOOL BOX

During the first semester after Covid 19 hit the world in March 2020, college instructors (and likely most teachers) were challenged with how to best engage our students in an all-online platform during our classes. I will never forget the class where my new engagement strategy seemed to be working for most of my students, as they happily posted, chatted and volunteered their answers. However, there was one student who stayed quiet throughout the entire class. When I was able to check in with her, after this class, I mentioned how I noticed she was not very participatory in class and I asked her if everything was ok. She replied, "Yes everything is fine. I wanted to participate but I just find it easier to stay quiet." This comment prompted a great conversation between us about the balance of class engagement, listening and staying quiet when you have something to say.

Too often we may find it easier, or at least more comfortable, to stay quiet. Now I fully understand why my student felt more apt to stay quiet. She was already self-conscious about speaking in front of others. Now we have a new platform which changed everything about how we communicate as a class, so her response was understandable. However, this occurrence led me to think about all the times women stay quiet because it just feels more comfortable. More often, this may be the case because we are not sure what to say, how to say it and if we should even say anything. Then, you pile on the human nature's fear of being judged, or feeling different and we are lucky if we even show up for that class/appointment/meeting/event!

My Communication Studies class not only explores public speaking, which every college student loves, just like slow Wi-Fi, we also discuss preparing for the unexpected. They often question me on how that is even possible. This is when we discuss their potential questions from customers at their place of work, or when their supervisor leans on them to explain a process to their peers during a staff meeting, or when their professor calls on them to contribute to class discussion about the week's required reading; because it may not be expected, this becomes an impromptu communication situation. Too often, people assume that you cannot prepare for the unexpected but that is untrue. It is important to be prepared for the situations you do not necessarily see coming. It is also possible, but it is also the trick that may just be the secret ingredient to your Big Girl Pants confidence!

For example, I often think about what potential topics may arise when I find myself in a meeting. Not only do I try to prepare for the obvious, i.e. the purpose of my presence at the meeting, but I also think about three other topics someone could question me about and three potential points of consternation I may need to combat. Then, I prepare phrases or what I like to label 'communication tools' that I keep in my figurative back pocket so I will be prepared.

The reason for this tool box is because too many decisions made on the spot often cause us to stop and under-communicate; that is, communicate in a way that is below our best level. The result is that we tend to take the easiest or most comfortable path in reacting to others. When we under-communicate, it is usually at the expense of demonstrating our value, worth, our boundaries and most often, our confidence. If you prepare ahead of time and become familiar with phrases before you need them, you are more apt to state them at the right time with confidence. One way I have learned to combat this hesitancy to participate and speak up, is via a Communication Toolbox.

WHAT IS A COMMUNICATION TOOLBOX?

A communication toolbox is full of phrases as tools, that you might need in the future. You create these phrases before you actually need them. You prepare ahead of time when your head is clear, when you do not have all eyes on you, and when you are not expected to react.

My Communication Toolbox was started in adolescence, if I think all the way back. There was a group of girls who set their sights on me when it came to sarcastic comments meant to insult. I remember gearing myself up in the morning as I was getting ready for school, by anticipating what their remarks may be, then creating a response or a comeback. I'd think of a few options and settle on one phrase or sentence that I liked the most. Then I repeated it a few times until I had it down for the day. While this sounds like a lot of work, I kind of liked exploring the best way to communicate my boundaries. I was simply preparing for the unexpected. I could not know exactly who would approach me or what would come out of their mouths. But I could bank on someone trying to engage. Those preemptive comebacks helped me to gain confidence. I see now that it gave me the self-assuredness to walk into school, knowing if someone wanted to try to get a rise out of me, I already had a phrase ready to go, to respond. And bonus – since I had spent time thinking about my phrase, it was usually a good comeback. (I now would like to thank my parents, for their impeccable usage of sarcasm.) Eventually, the girls stopped approaching me with snarky remarks. Of course, looking back now, I realize this was all just part of the growing up experience. We were all doing what we needed to, to survive and find our own value and worth among the challenges of our teen years. And actually, I likely owe these girls for teaching me to verbally defend myself. Ladies, if we ever exchanged words in high school, I formally thank you right here and now.

Have you ever found yourself in a situation where you stayed quiet because you did not know what to say at the time? Instead of wishing you could have had a good comeback, question or comment, you can actually prepare for the unexpected.

HOW DOES THIS TOOLBOX WORK?

When we find ourselves in a situation where we are not quite sure what to say, we become overwhelmed in the moment with having to make so many decisions on the spot. It then becomes easier to say nothing. However, if we already have our phraseology, in a toolbox at the ready, the decision now becomes easier. If you know the actual words and phrases and you are familiar with the content of your response, then the decision is when to speak up not if you should speak. By having phrases prepared, you take a lot of the work out of making your presence or voice known. Below you will see some examples of these phrases. However, each of us, experience very unique situations both at work, school and our personal lives so the exact phrases will be uniquely tied to your own experience. And as we grow and our situations change, our phrases will evolve. (And if you ever want to brainstorm with me... meg@megbucaro.com)

Thankfully, I no longer rely on the tools of my teen years. However, I do need to whip one of my communication tools out when a meeting is getting off track and we need to stay on time. Or when a person has hijacked the speaking time during a meeting and we need to move on. I may utilize the "Dana, that is an excellent point and for now, to be respectful of everyone's time, let's get back to XYZ before our time together ends." Also, it is important to do what we can to prepare phrases that we are comfortable enough with saying, at a moment's notice. This is the concept of a communication toolbox.

COMMUNICATION TOOLS: THE PHRASES

Let's say you deal with a difficult person on a regular basis and never quite know what may fly out of their mouth. You may ignore their comments because you do not want to deal with them and/or hate to be too confrontational. However, they are out of line or rude. You wish you could say something to create a boundary. In the past, you wouldn't mind drawing a little attention to their behavior so they don't continue to act in this manner. However, you can't seem to ever predict how they may offend. After thinking it through proactively, you place the following phrases in your communication toolbox;

- To clarify, I just heard this _____ is this in line with what you meant?
- Can you please explain it further?
- Tell me more...
- Wow. (PAUSE), please tell me more about that.

By your comment, you are respectfully showing recognition of their offensive communication. By addressing their comments, you are stating a boundary by not letting their rude comments fly by you without a reaction.

Next, let's say a colleague asks you a question and you do not know what your answer should be. You do not want to look stupid as if you do not know the answer. You may not want to say "I don't know." So instead you have the following in your communication toolbox:

- I do not have an answer for you right now, let me get back to you.
- I am not sure how I feel about that right now, let me get back to you.
- That is interesting and I need more time to think this through... let me circle back with you.

- I would like a bit of time to process this request, I will circle back with you as I don't have the answer for you right now.

These are just a few options of endless possibilities. The key to creating the phrases in your tool box is to make sure you can see yourself using them. Make the phrases your own.

Another example may be in a situation where someone is questioning your authority or your decisions. Instead of being rattled, shutting down or showing that you are bothered, you may say something like:

- Why do you ask?

- Did I do something to offend you? (Just seems like you are having an unusual interest in my reasoning right now, maybe I am sensing this wrongly?)

- Jean, (important to use their name), what do you think about XYZ situation? If this person has a grudge for some reason, they may like being asked for their opinion. All you have to say is, "Thank you, something to consider…" as a response.

The point after these few examples is that you have endless opportunities to develop your own sayings. If you are reading this book with others, this is a great discussion question. Make a list of communication situations where you could benefit from a list of pre-determined phrases. Discuss and brainstorm what those phrases may sound like coming out of your mouth. Be realistic and don't stop until you found a few viable options.

ACTION ITEM:
CREATE YOUR COMMUNICATION TOOLBOX

1. **Identify the situations.** When do you want to be able to confidently speak up? Reflect why you have not spoken up in the past.

I suggest physically listing the situations that you experienced. Describe what happened as well as your feelings in that moment.

2. **Address any concerns**. Is speaking up out of your comfort zone? Does someone intimidate you so you just don't want to deal with them? Is there a power dynamic that makes you uncomfortable? Dive into these concerns, owning your feelings and being as objective as possible knowing the end goal is creating phrases that you can own and will use.

3. **Create the phrases.** List every single possible phrase. Create a list template. Highlight a potential situation as a header, then list the phrases you can use during that type of situation below it. Review it. Update it. Have it at the ready. This is your Communication Toolbox.

4. **Practice.** Become so familiar with these phrases that they roll off your tongue. You do *not* want the first few times you say the phrase to be when it really counts. Practice. Rehearse. Record yourself. Watch the video. As silly as it sounds you are simply rehearsing so you feel more comfortable and confident when the time is right to pull out the right tool.

BOTTOM LINE

The more prepared you are for the most unexpected situations, the more confident you will feel. The more confident you feel, the better you show up to the best of your ability and authentically so. Do not under-communicate just because you have not taken the time to prepare yourself. We are judged constantly on how we show up in various settings. Do not leave your presence to chance. Prepare by proactively creating your communication toolbox to present your best self, even in the most unexpected situations.

CHAPTER 8:

THE BEST VERSION OF YOURSELF -YOUR BIG GIRL PANTS-

You have the power within to achieve the success you desire, however you define it! You are smarter, more beautiful and stronger than you actually believe. It is high time to start communicating as if you know your incredible value. When we put on our 'big girl pants' we sit in our significant worth and demonstrate our beautiful and unique gifts that only we possess. We don't do this for show but we authentically know ourselves and are not going to be intimidated to shrink, take up less verbal or physical space and make ourselves smaller. Knowing we are valuable and worthy does not mean we are egotistical or fake. Our big girl pants have everything to do with becoming and showing up as the best version of ourselves. Confidently presenting yourself is both exhilarating and possible. I believe there is no better time than now to greet the world and those around you with your best!

THE PERFECTION CONUNDRUM

Before you put down this book, the perfectionists of the world must be lovingly addressed, and they may need to sit down for this one... the goal is never perfection. Perfection is for robots not humans. It is impossible for human beings who are intrinsically flawed, to be perfect. I understand your desire for things to be just right. I understand your desire for the job to be completed to the absolute best of your ability and even, for those of us who enjoy a little competition, better than others! However, if we constantly strive for perfection, we will often be disappointed. If our focus is to be completely flawless, we come up short more often than not. Communication is as much art as it is a science and there is no perfection in the art of communication. Our goal is always to strive for progress not perfection. While our world certainly benefits from artificial intelligence, expressing ourselves as our best does not mean we should turn into robots that will never take a misstep. In fact, I will argue that trying to be perfect does more damage to our self-worth than any negative self-talk. Why set perfection as the bar that must be reached when you can simply encourage yourself to be your best? Your best measures differently among each individual. There is no need to compete. I have a dear friend who is great at ensuring a process gets done efficiently and effectively. The details of a process are not my strong suit. (Don't even talk to me about the intricate details of Chicago Manual of Style bibliography format.#smh) However, my friend helps me with a process I find challenging and I help her build her communication tool box with creative phrases for various situations. We don't compare ourselves to each other's best. We focus on doing our own best.

I encourage you to spend your energy on the strategies written in this book to put your big girl pants on and strive to show up as the best version of yourself. Strive to strengthen your communication muscles. Believe in yourself. Believe that you are capable. Then envision your success. But do not have 'perfection' as the goal.

WHEN THE BIG GIRLS PANTS ARE UNCOMFORTABLE

While I was writing this book, I posted a formatting request in a private Facebook group. I was seeking very specific citation formatting assistance (I told you I wasn't a detailed gal). Knowing that citation styling is not a strong suit of mine, I thought about hiring a woman from the group who may have expertise in this area. I explained the concept of the book, the process that I was currently working through with my editors and publisher and explained the purpose of my request. What I received were unsolicited opinions of my book, the title, the working book cover and the general concept. I graciously thanked the posters for their attention and enthusiasm but reiterated the purpose of my request was for a specific citation formatting not generalized opinions. They could not help themselves. More comments, lending opinions that had nothing to do with my request. I could have believed them. I could have interacted, responded to their comments and questioned why they thought so negatively about certain aspects of this book. I could have asked them for suggestions. I could have sought their approval. However, I realized, they had not earned the right to offer their opinions because they were not my editor nor publisher and bottom line, I never asked for their opinions on my book content. Frankly, their opinions were more about themselves than they were about my book. I, once again, put my big girl pants on and dismissed their comments, after withdrawing my request. It became obvious that I was not going to get assistance on my request so it was time to move along, knowing my own value of my ideas and my book. (Now, when my editor offers suggestions, you bet your bottom dollar I listen!) Clearly, at times we will likely come up against a force that is not for us. Does not like our strength. Will not appreciate our confidence. When this occurs, remember their opinion is more about them than you.

Putting your big girl pants on will not always be easy or feel comfortable but that is precisely how you will know you are expanding and growing.

In fact, when you have these feelings of uncomfortability, I'd challenge you to view them as growing pains, a sign that you are growing into your big girl pants, growing in confidence and self-assuredness. Put your big girls pants on, be your best and stand in your worth and confidence. Take up space, expand your shoulders, lift your chin and feel the strength of your voice. Our world needs you. Our world needs your gifts. Always remember, our world needs you to put your big girl pants on and be comfortable being the best version of yourself, regardless how uncomfortable that makes others. As the American actress, screenwriter and producer Mindy Kaling says, "...the scary thing I have noticed is that some people really feel uncomfortable around women who don't hate themselves." If you are busy doing your best, remember other's opinions are not really your business. Their opinion is their business.

So as I said in the first chapter of this book, let this book be a call to arms to fight the self-doubt, rejection, or stumbling blocks that has stopped or slowed you down from pursuing what you know is your future success. The world will continue to throw difficult situations at us, but we must promise ourselves to utilize the tools we have to push ourselves towards whatever we define as success! Then, we must fight like hell to stay on that path with our big girls pants on, taking up our rightful space. Take what you've learned from this book and show the world the very best version of the bad ass woman reading this book!

BIBLIOGRAPHY

CHAPTER 1:

1 "The 3 Trends Transforming How Your People Connect." Video Communication Trends Report. Ebook. Quantified Communications, 2021.

2 Vatansever, D., Menon, D. K., and Stamatakis, E. A. "Default Mode Contributions to Automated Information Processing." Proceedings of the National Academy of Sciences of the United States of America 114, no. 48 (2017): 12821-12826. Accessed June 23, 2023 https://doi.org/10.1073/pnas.1710521114.

3 Amos, Julie-Ann. "Body Language Differences between Men and Women." Body Language Expert UK. June 18, 2017.

4 Nelson, Audrey, Ph.D. "Difference in Nonverbal Cues Between Men and Women." Psychology Today. March 15, 2022.

CHAPTER 2:

5 Ambady, Nalini and Robert Rosenthal. "Thin Slices of Expressive Behaviors as Predictors of Interpersonal Consequences: A Meta-Analysis." Psychological Bulletin 111, no. 2 (1992): 256-274.

6 Ambady, Nalini, and Robert Rosenthal. "Thin Slices of Expressive Behavior as Predictors of Interpersonal Consequences: A Meta-Analysis." Psychological Bulletin 111, no. 2 (1992): 256-274.

7 Nelson, Audrey, PhD. "Differences in Nonverbal Cues Between Men and Women." Psychology Today, March 15, 2022.

8 Weisbuch, Max, Nalini Ambady, Asha L. Clarke, and Sawn Actor. "On Being Consistent: The Role of Verbal-Nonverbal Consistency in First Impressions." Basic and Applied Social Physiology 32 (2010): 261-268.

9 Ambady, Nalini and Robert Rosenthal. "Thin Slices of Expressive Heavier as Predictors of Interpersonal Consequences: A Meta Analysis." Psychological Bulletin 111, no. 2 (1992): 256-274.

CHAPTER 3:

10 "Dictionary Oxford Languages, Accessed June 23, 2023 https://languages.oup.com/google-dictionary-en/

11 "Building Confidence," KidsHealth, Accessed May 14, 2022, https://kidshealth.org/en/teens/confidence.html.

12 "Confidence," Psychology Today, Accessed May 14, 2022, https://www.psychologytoday.com/us/basics/confidence.

13 Kay, Katty and Shipman, Claire. The Confidence Code: The Science and Art of Self-Assurance – What Women Should Know (New York: Harper Business, 2014).

14 Mehta, Kumar, "The Superpower of Confidence," Forbes, Accessed May 12, 2022, https://www.forbes.com/sites/kmehta/2022/05/12/the-superpower-of-confidence/?sh=3e2236357ee8.

15 Cuso, Nina and Tyler, Michael "How to Be More Confident by Appearance, Self-Confidence, Competition," April 12, 2019. Accessed May 15, 2022 https://community.thriveglobal.com/how-to-be-more-confident-by-appearance-self-confidence-competition-and-of-course-nina-cuso/

16 Kay, Katty and Shipman, Claire. The Confidence Code: The Science and Art of Self-Assurance - What Women Should Know (New York: Harper Business, 2014).

17 Ambady, Nalini, Mary Anne Krabbenhoft, and Daniel Hogan. "The 30-Sec. Scale: Using Thin-Slice Judgements to Evaluate Sales Effectiveness," Journal of Consumer Psychology 16, no. 1 (2006): 4-13.

18 Maxwell, John C. "Must the Confidence and Responsibility: And Master the Cornerstone of Leadership," Success, February 2010.

19 American Confidence Institute, "Why Are We Attracted to Confidence?" Accessed May 15, 2022, https://www.americanconfidenceinstitute.com/blog/why-we-are-attracted-to-confidence#:~:text=Confidence%20continuously%20tops%20the%20lists,we%20are%20attracted%20to%20confidence.

20 Krause, Sascha, Mitja D. Back, Boris Egloff, and Stefan C. Schmuukle. "Predicting Self-Confident Behavior with Implicit and Explicit Self Esteem Measures." University of Leipzig, Germany. European Journal of Personalist 30 (2016): 648-662. Published October 5, 2016.

21 Markway, Barbara, "Why Self-Confidence Is More Important Than You Think," Psychology Today, Accessed September 25, 2018, https://www.psychologytoday.com/us/blog/shyness-is-nice/201809/why-self-confidence-is-more-important-you-think

CHAPTER 4:

22 Cuddy, Amy. "When the Revolution Came for Amy Cuddy." *The New York Times Magazine,* October 18, 2017. https://www.nytimes.com/2017/10/18/magazine/when-the-revolution-came-for-amy-cuddy.html. Accessed August 9, 2023.

23 Cuddy, Amy. "When the Revolution Came for Amy Cuddy." *The New York Times Magazine,* October 18, 2017. https://www.nytimes.com/2017/10/18/magazine/when-the-revolution-came-for-amy-cuddy.html. Accessed August 9, 2023

24 Carney, Dana R., Amy J. Cuddy, and Andy J. Yap, "Power Posing: Brief Nonverbal Displays Affect Neuroendocrine Levels and Risk Tolerance," Psychological Science 21, no. 10 (2010): 1363-1368, https://doi.org/10.1177/0956797610383437

25 Cuddy, Amy, website, accessed May 15, 2022, https://www.amycuddy.com/

CHAPTER 5:

26 Mohindra, Vinita, and Samina Aznar, "Gender Communication: A Comparative Analysis of Communicational Approaches of Men and Women at Workplaces," IOSR Journal of Humanities and Social Sciences 2, no. 1 (2012): 10-16.

27 Not Inferior – Quote Investigator." Quote Investigator. Accessed March 2, 202. https://quoteinvestigator.com/2011/03/30/not-inferior/

28 Shames, Deborah, "Speak Up! A Woman's Guide to Presenting Like A Pro," Thrive Global, March 27, 2017, https://medium.com/thrive-global/what-holds-women-back-from-becoming-strong-public-speakers-5a27f-0cc6deb

29 Maxey, Cyndi, and Kevin O'Connor, Speak Up! A Woman's Guide to Presenting Like A Pro (Santa Barbara: Praeger, 2018).

30 Dwyer, Karen Kansas, and Howe Davidson, Marlina Marie. "The Influence of Diaphragmatic Breathing to Reduce Anxiety for Basic Course Students." Communication Education 56, no. 2 (2007): 206-222.

31 . Dwyer, Karen Kansas, and Howe Davidson, Marlina Marie. "The Influence of Diaphragmatic Breathing to Reduce Anxiety for Basic Course Students." Communication Education 56, no. 2 (2007): 206-222

32 Bucaro Wojtas, Meg. Gender Difference in the Communication of Confidence. 2019. Elgin Community College Faculty Research Cohort report.